A JEWISH TALE

THE CHRONICLES OF A JEWISH REBEL
AND HOW SHE WAS CONQUERED
BY THE PRINCE OF PEACE

ELIZABETH COOPER

Copyright © 2022 Elizabeth Cooper

All rights reserved. No part of this book may be reproduced, stored, or transmitted by any means—whether auditory, graphic, mechanical, or electronic—without written permission of both publisher and author, except in the case of brief excerpts used in critical articles and reviews. Unauthorized reproduction of any part of this work is illegal and is punishable by law.

Scripture quotations are taken from the following sources
The Holy Bible. New International Version (NIV).
Copyright©1973, 1978, 1984 by International Bible Society.

Complete Jewish Bible.
Copyright©1998 by David H. Stern, published by Jewish New Testament Publications, Inc.

The Holy Bible, New King James Version (NKJV).
Copyright©1982 by Thomas Nelson, Inc.

The Holy Scriptures. The Masoretic Text.
Copyright© 1917 by the Jewish Publication Society of America.

ISBN: 978-1-957203-11-9 (sc)
ISBN: 978-1-957203-12-6 (hc)
ISBN: 978-1-957203-13-3 (e)

Because of the dynamic nature of the Internet, any web addresses or links contained in this book may have changed since publication and may no longer be valid. The views expressed in this work are solely those of the author and do not necessarily reflect the views of the publisher, and the publisher hereby disclaims any responsibility for them.

The Ewings Publishing LLC
One Galleria Blvd., Suite 1900, Metairie, LA 70001
1-888-421-2397

CONTENTS

Acknowledgements 1
Introduction 3
My Roots 5
Try Politics 8
Israel—My Destiny? 10
Political Activism 12
The Counterculture 14
The Eastern Wave 17
The Supernatural 19
Coming Into The Light 21
Growing in Knowledge 24
The One 28
Jesus is Jewish 29
Miryam's Song 32
Return Home 34
Love and Marriage 36
The Children 40
Fires and Floods 43
Back to Teaching 47
Special Education 49
Cancer 52
The Fall 55
Restoration 57
Amazing Love 59
Afterword 61
Two Women 63
Appendix 65
The Promised Land 76

ACKNOWLEDGEMENTS

Special thanks to my dear sisters, MaryAnn Murray and Jan Edelman, who stuck by me for four years typing and editing this work. Without their labor of love this book would not have come to be.

And thanks to my husband, Jeffrey, whose encouragement helped me to persevere until the end.

My gratitude also goes to Marianne Pizzo, Ellen Presser, and Greg Anglen for their kindness in helping me get this work published.

INTRODUCTION

This book is a memoir of the spiritual journey of an American Jewess, who at the age of twenty-eight had an encounter with the God of Abraham, Isaac and Jacob through the Jewish Messiah, Jesus (Yeshua).

I learned of my Redeemer in 1973, but the realization that Jesus was Jewish occurred two years later after reading the biographies of two other Jewish believers.

I rejoiced in the knowledge that I didn't have to change from what I was. I was still a Jew and Christianity is Jewish, because Jesus is the Messiah!

In the last forty years, through the forgiveness received by the atoning work of the Messiah, I have come to know the great Creator God, the God of the Bible, and the God of my Fathers. He, through the Messiah, allows people to speak to Him directly, that is, to have a personal relationship with Him. He is the One who led me to my husband, and to my career. In addition, He has also given me the strength to endure the difficult challenges that have occurred in my life.

Through the years, I have come to know more of the God who told Abraham to go to a place that will be shown to him; and to Moses He revealed that it was time to deliver the people of Israel, and God was going to use him. He's the One who also gave Joseph supernatural understanding of Pharaoh's dreams leading to the deliverance of Israel.

Today, that same God still empowers, leads and purifies a people who have the desire to know and serve Him as King of Kings and Lord of Lords.

A walk of faith is not easy. It is hard to trust in a God you do not see. But when you experience the changes He makes in your heart, see answers to prayer, and, know peace as you live according to His will you comprehend that He is real and that He loves and cares for those who enter into a covenant relationship with Him, through Yeshua, the Messiah.

MY ROOTS

My parents were second generation Jewish Americans. In the early twentieth century, their parents came to the United States from Russia and Poland. They went through the formidable experience of being processed at Ellis Island, as new immigrants to the United States of America.

Both my parents grew up in Brooklyn. My father's parents were Orthodox Jews, following closely to religious traditions; while my mother's family was Conservative, not adhering as strictly to religious practices.

Soon after my parents were married they moved to Rockaway Beach, a seaside community in Queens. Since they both had enjoyed swimming there in their youth, they decided it would be a pleasant place to raise a family.

Not long after moving to Rockaway, a friendly neighbor invited my parents to visit her Reformed temple. They went, liked the people they met, and chose to become members.

Thus, I grew up in a Reformed Jewish home. In temple the men and women sat together; the services were mostly in English; the men didn't wear yamulkas (head coverings); and the families didn't keep kosher dietary laws. From a religious point of view, we believed in the Ten Commandments, and Almighty God, who may have personally intervened in people's lives in Old Testament days but not in modern times.

Fear was an underlying presence in our home growing up. Fear of the world at large; fear of differences; and a fear of anti-Semitism. Consequently, my family lived in a mostly Jewish neighborhood, and my sister and I went to predominantly Jewish schools. We felt safer with the familiar.

My family was active in our temple. When I was young, my mother served as a volunteer Sunday school secretary. Later, she went on staff as the temple bookkeeper for many years.

As a child, I was also involved in various temple activities. I participated in Purim parades where the children dressed up in costumes depicting the characters from the book of Esther. Then during Passover I went to see the Rabbi conduct a model *Seder,* the ceremonial Passover dinner, where he explained the symbolism of the different elements on the *Seder* plate. At Hanukkah I would sing songs that retold the stirring story of the great victory of the Israelite, Judah Maccabee, over the occupying Assyrian army.

Not only did I participate in celebrating the Jewish holidays, but every Saturday morning from the time I was six, I sang in the religious school choir which accompanied the Rabbi during the Sabbath morning services. This involvement in temple life gave me a strong identification with my Jewish heritage, and added color and rhythm to an otherwise typical, middle-class American childhood of the 1950s.

By far, the best part of growing up in Rockaway was the summers at the beach, where I'd be transformed into a water sprite.

Almost every summer morning, we would pack a bag with our lunch, towels and sunscreen, and hike the "three" long blocks to the beach. Upon arrival, after spreading our blanket on the sand, and laying everything else on it, I'd run down to the water and stay there for the rest of the day, except when hunger pangs could not be ignored.

Most of the hours at the ocean were filled with jumping waves, or later when I got older, body surfing--riding the waves into the shore on my stomach. It was an exciting challenge trying to catch the crest of a wave at just the right moment. For a change of pace, my friends and I would make sand castles by packing sand higher and higher, then dribbling wet sand between our fingers to make delicate spires.

While digging in the wet sand, we often found sand crabs of different sizes. We delighted in digging them up, then putting them down on the beach to watch them scamper away, and suddenly stop, and burrow back in the sand.

Being at the beach on those steamy, hot days was a terrific way to spend my summers. Back then, I thought most kids did the same thing. Later I realized those days at the beach had been a great privilege.

For recreation at other times of the year, I enjoyed practicing my roller skating skills. I was a sight skating around and around in circles, trying to emulate the stars I saw in the Roller Derby matches on TV. When there were enough kids to play, my neighbors and I would get a game of punch ball or stickball going in the street.

On my block, the children of the Jewish families and Irish families played together freely. However, I, personally, felt there was a wall of separation between us. I was reacting to the statues of Mary or the Holy Family my Irish neighbors had on their lawns. From my Jewish upbringing, I was familiar with the commandment about not having any graven images before you (Deuteronomy 5:8). As a child, I assumed my neighbors worshipped these statues which in my eyes made them idolaters and, therefore, lesser people.

It took some years for that wall of prejudice against my Irish neighbors to come down. It occurred when I was about twenty.

On a sunny, Saturday afternoon, I went to see a baseball game played among a bunch of fellows (Jewish and Irish young men) from the neighborhood. After the game, we all went for some refreshments.

As we enjoyed socializing, I realized that the Irish young people were just like me! What an eye opener and a freeing experience—a wall of prejudice had come down.

About that time, I was teaching kindergarten in the temple's Sunday School. One Sunday morning, we were learning about Joseph and how he had interpreted Pharaoh's dream concerning the seven fat cows (seven years of prosperity), and seven lean cows (seven years of famine). The story quickened something within my heart. I went to the Sunday School principal and asked him how Joseph was able to explain the dreams.

His reply was, "Well, you know how psychiatrists like Freud interpret dreams. Joseph had similar abilities".

His answer was significant to me because, subconsciously, it was then that I knew, I had to seek elsewhere, (other than my Reformed Jewish background), for the answers to life's mysteries.

TRY POLITICS

Taking a step towards independence just before my twenty first birthday, I moved from my parent's home to an apartment in Manhattan. A few months earlier, I had also begun teaching in an inner-city elementary school.

I found teaching to be a challenge for which I was not prepared. But, it wasn't the children themselves that caused me to feel ill-equipped for the job. Rather, I felt there was something missing within me.

Having lived a sheltered middle-class life, I thought I didn't know enough about life and the world to be the role model the children needed. After a year I quit teaching and got a job as a publicity assistant in a book publishing company.

Outwardly, it seemed I had not fared well at my first teaching assignment. But, inwardly, upon reflection, I knew a good thing had happened; growth as a person had occurred. I had loved children of a different race, and thus, the unconscious barrier of racial prejudice had fallen.

While living in the city, I also started to get politically active. In my one year of teaching in the inner city, I had seen enough of the effects of inequality to want to try to do something about it. It was also apparent that I was hearkening to my father's teachings. As my father, a lifelong Democrat, would read the daily newspaper, he would comment on the political issues of the day. He was convinced that the political process was the only way to change society for the better. I, therefore, took up his point of view, and began to get involved.

I aligned myself with the Reform Democratic Club because the candidates it supported were not tied to the New York City Democratic machine of the late 1960s. However, the political activity along traditional party lines, of attending meetings and making phone calls in support of our candidates, was not the road I would travel on for very long.

The Vietnam War era had begun, and I was soon swept into the serge of the youthful anti-war protests. My involvement in the anti-war movement began when I left New York City.

Having a desire to renew a relationship with a young man I had been seeing for several years, I moved upstate to Buffalo, New York, where he was attending school. Soon after I arrived, I obtained a job teaching, once again, in the inner city.

ISRAEL—MY DESTINY?

In the summer of 1969, after teaching my first year in Buffalo, I went to Israel, primarily, to attend the wedding of a high school friend. I also wanted to see if there was something about Israel, related to my being Jewish, that would stir my soul. I traveled there with a tour group of Jewish American young people.

While in Israel we visited such well-known places as the old city of Jerusalem, the Dead Sea, and Masada, a famous site of Israeli resistance in the war against Rome. We also enjoyed hiking in the woods in Ein Gedi, an oasis near the Negev Desert; and for a week, we lived and worked on a kibbutz--a cooperative farming community--picking peaches from six to eleven in the morning. (I still remember how itchy my arms were from the peach fuzz!) Then finally, I went to celebrate my friend Elaine's wedding.

There were two notable things that happened on that trip. God gave me glimpses of Himself through His creation. For example, one day, I happened to look into a flower, and I marveled at its vivid colors and the perfection of its design. I thought, "Man's creative efforts are mere copies of God's handiwork." Then on the night of my birthday, I was lying on the beach at Eilat, the southern-most city in Israel, on the Gulf of Aqaba, gazing up at the stars. Suddenly, there was a meteor shower; meteors were shooting about in every direction! It was the most spectacular thing I had ever seen. I mused, "God has given me a very special birthday gift this night."

When it was time to leave Israel, I knew it was not the place for me. While I had relished seeing its historic places and enjoyed experiencing the pungent aromas and tastes of the Middle Eastern cultures in the old city of Jerusalem, I realized that most Israelis, though very courageous, were agnostics who embraced western consumerism. I, therefore, didn't view their philosophy as being very different from mine and what I was gradually turning away from. I was ready to go home.

POLITICAL ACTIVISM

After returning to Buffalo in the fall of 1969, I was given my new teaching assignment. It was a class of more than 30 fifth-graders most of whom were performing two years below grade level.

In a short time, I realized that the books I was given to use with the class were inappropriate. The children couldn't read them, or the questions relating to the material within the books. As their teacher, I was terribly frustrated, but soon learned that the administration was not open to hear about, or deal with my concerns. Consequently, I began to look elsewhere to try to change a situation I knew wasn't right.

Having gained some political awareness, I became actively involved with both a social action committee of the Buffalo Teachers' Union, and the Parents' Association (P.A.) in my school.

Within the Teachers' Union, I was among a core of four or five teachers who were working on a proposal to integrate the Buffalo public schools, as one means of improving the education in the African-American community.

In my school, I began speaking with and encouraging the P.A. President (whose son was in my class), to try to get the parents more involved in the school. Hopefully, with more parental participation, the administration would be motivated to find out the reasons why the children were so far behind, and then discover strategies that could be used to remedy the situation.

My sentiments and activities did not go unnoticed. After more than 1 1/2 years I was asked to resign.

I was upset and frustrated with a system that failed children, and that the people in charge did not want to change it. Therefore, when the winds of more radical political approaches arose on the scene in Buffalo, I was ready and eager to take part.

Now having free time, I began spending my days on the campus of the University of Buffalo, where I found some consolation with other young people with like-minded ideals—equal rights and justice for all.

As an observer on campus, I would, for example, sit in on a large meeting of women students who spoke about "Women's Liberation", and the sisterhood of all women. At the time, I felt a great sense of relief knowing there were women who no longer felt they had to be in competition with one another to attract the male population. Instead, their purpose was to work together for the betterment of the under-represented groups of people in our society, including women. In addition, I would also pass by the office of the Students for a Democratic Society (S.D.S.), and learn how these students looked to the social movements in Latin America and China as models for their political aspirations—the unity of all working class people and their rise to political power. Thus, I was getting my feet wet with those who had a more wide-reaching political agenda.

The pinnacle of my political activities in Buffalo occurred in the spring of 1970. The anti-Vietnam War fervor on campus had been growing. Every day in outdoor rallies, speakers talked against the war. Finally, one day it was decided to have a demonstration in downtown Buffalo.

On the day planned, many students and I marched from the campus toward the heart of the city. We were chanting our slogans and some were throwing rocks. We hadn't gotten very far before the police appeared and started to toss tear gas in our midst. Unfortunately for the students, the tear gas did its job as the marchers quickly scattered.

Days later these demonstrators took over the various buildings on campus. They sat in, slept in, and effectively closed down the University of Buffalo campus for the rest of the Spring 1970 semester.

In June 1970, the spring semester ended, and the students left for the summer. I had broken up with my boyfriend and didn't have a job. My friend and I felt we had had enough of Buffalo, New York, and what we viewed as its resistance to social change. So after some deliberation, we decided to leave, and go West, to the area of the nation where the "CULTURAL REVOLUTION" had begun.

THE COUNTERCULTURE

It was on a bright summer day in 1970, when Maureen and I loaded up her red MGB convertible and bid farewell to New York state.

Since Buffalo is situated near the Canadian border, we planned a rather circuitous route. Instead of going directly west, we decided to take a horseshoe shaped course through Ontario, in order to visit all of its provincial parks.

During our many stops in Ontario, we felt like the early explorers who were the first to witness the pristine beauty of this exquisite land with its dense evergreen forests and sparkling lakes.

But alas, after camping out for a week and a half, it was back to civilization, as we arrived in Bozeman, Montana where Maureen's cousins lived. After staying a few days, Maureen decided to remain and try to set down some roots in Bozeman.

However, the West Coast was drawing me. I decided to continue on to the San Francisco Bay area in northern California, where I had a friend and cousins that had settled there several years before.

When I arrived in the Bay Area, I visited my cousins in San Francisco, but went to stay temporarily at my high school friend's home in Berkeley. My friend Judy and her husband Sandy had started a small alternative school in Berkeley. They graciously let me stay with them until I got my own place.

One day as I was "hanging out" on the U. C. campus at Berkeley I noticed a young man giving out political flyers. We began to talk. He told me he was involved with an anarchist collective, and that the group was living in a commune in Berkeley. He invited me to take a look at the place, to see if I would want to live there. I was interested, and found the address he gave me without difficulty.

The commune consisted of two side-by-side three story residential houses. Each member of the collective had a room and shared the living room and kitchen. After walking around and meeting some of the residents, I decided to move in.

As anarchists, the group did not have any regular meetings; although among ourselves, we did get together and have some lively discussions. Most of the residents were engaged in their own political activities within the Berkeley community.

In the Bay Area, by the summer of 1970 the peak of the more volatile political protests had passed. The Bank of America in Berkeley had previously been set on fire, and several leaders of the Black Panther party had already been arrested.

Now the "revolutionary" community mobilized to create a self-sufficient counterculture to mainstream America, one that didn't depend on the mega corporations. This endeavor took various forms in Berkeley.

First, many of the young people chose to live collectively to reduce their expenses. Most of these communes had their own gardens. To purchase other necessary food items, a "Food Conspiracy" was formed. The people on each block organized to purchase food once a week from the Farmer's Market in San Francisco.

After the run to San Francisco, the food would be brought to one home, and each neighbor would go there to pick up his order. The block members took turns picking up the produce from the Farmer's Market.

Berkeley had a free health clinic staffed by volunteers. The doctors and nurses who served there also related to the cause of creating an alternative community. The parents in the community established a system of cooperative day care amongst themselves, and whoever else was interested in helping them.

During this period, I read Eldridge Cleaver's <u>Soul on Ice</u>, and embraced the liberation struggle Mr. Cleaver endorsed. Subsequently, several friends and I, joined the White Panthers, which was the white extension of the Black Panther Party.

By this time, however, the Black Panthers themselves were undergoing a change. Much of their activity now focused on helping to improve the lives of the people in their community. They began to feed people in need, tutor children, and organize classes to train people in different self-help skills.

Through their classes, I learned simple plumbing techniques, and had a bit of success hanging windows. In addition, I took up crocheting. One of my first projects was to crochet black berets, (a symbol of the Black Panthers) for several of us.

I was feeling good about becoming more self-reliant, but my funds were running low. Consequently, I began to seek more consistent employment.

My first steady job was in Oakland, selling yard goods at a fabric store. When the store closed, I commuted across the bay to San Francisco to work full-time for New York Life Insurance Company, in the customer service department.

When I first started working there, I felt like I was working for the enemy, but regardless, I had to eat! As time went on, I began to like the camaraderie among the large pool of women with whom I worked.

In the meantime, while my life had taken on a change of pace, commuting every day and working full time, another cultural shift was about to occur throughout the Bay Area.

THE EASTERN WAVE

By 1972, a strong wave from the Far East had reached the Bay Area, bringing with it teachers of Eastern philosophies.

The year before, the signs posted on the telephone poles in Berkeley announced meetings among various political action groups. Now, the signs proclaimed the arrival of the different popular Maharajas and Swamis of the day.

Coincidentally, at this time, I had had a personal revelation which caused me to also go in this new direction.

After living in the commune for over a year, I began to realize that my contemporaries, with their diverse political ideologies, would not be capable of creating a better society beyond the confines of Berkeley. There were several reasons that led me to this conclusion—namely, within the group I had seen clear evidence among a few members of racial intolerance, as well as, a high degree of drug usage (dependency, in some cases) impairing the user's judgment and ability to have a full life. Although I had also dabbled with drugs, many of the people I knew used them habitually.

Then along with this new understanding of the character of my peers came the realization that, before a man could create a better society, he had to change for the better on the inside--his heart had to change. It's an inside/out process.

Consequently, I began to probe into the Eastern philosophies with the hope of becoming a better "me". Many others in the community-at-large did this as well.

Thus, during that year, my friends and I attended large meetings, where the visiting Maharajas would speak. I also read several books on Hindu thought. Soon some of my friends began to align themselves with the different teachers, but I did not. No one teacher seemed to stand out to me.

A book that did make an impact on me, however, was Hermann Hesse's <u>Siddhartha.</u> Siddhartha's search for enlightenment inspired me not to give up, but to continue with my own personal quest.

One of the things I did glean from the different Hindu teachers however was the need to practice meditation. They explained that meditation would allow you to arrive at a more peaceful state of being, and thus be able to relate more harmoniously within your environment. Therefore, I decided to find out more about it, and met with the people at the Transcendental Meditation Center in Berkeley. Through them, I received a mantra and was taught their way of meditation.

At first, after meditating--sitting and repeating my mantra for about fifteen minutes a day--I would come away feeling more relaxed. But, several months later a change took place. I began to realize that when I meditated I was going into a deeper place in my consciousness, and something unknown was present. This presence did not reveal itself to me, and I was frightened by it. For that reason, I stopped meditating; it had become too unsettling. Later I learned, I had been calling to demonic beings, and they were responding to my invocations.

Not long after my experience with Transcendental Meditation, (TM), one of my friends invited me to a Spiritists' Church. It was there, that I first saw evidence of the supernatural realm operating in people's lives.

THE SUPERNATURAL

The first time I went to the Spiritists' Church, I had no idea what to expect.

When we arrived we were asked to write a question on a piece of paper related to something in our lives about which we wanted advice. We then folded our papers, put them into a basket, and took our seats. When the service began, the congregation sang some traditional Christian hymns. So far, this seemed normal to me.

Then a woman went to the podium, greeted everyone and started to give "readings"; that is, she began answering the questions on the papers that had been collected. Her method began in the following manner—she picked up a paper and stated facts relating to that person's life, whose paper she held. When she had given enough information so that the person knew she was addressing him or her, she then gave advice as to what should be done concerning the matter in question.

I was getting a little bored hearing information about people I didn't know, until suddenly, the woman began describing things pertaining to my life. She talked about places I'd been and things that I had done without fault. When she was sure she had my attention, without opening my paper, she proceeded to give advice relevant to my request. I was amazed. The woman had mentioned things about me, she had no natural way of knowing.

I was so affected by this phenomenon that I began to see one of the spiritists privately on a weekly basis, seeking guidance for my life.

After several months of attending the Spiritists' Church and having private readings, I started getting a buzzing sound in my ears. I knew that

I was being called to become a spiritist. Again, in fear of the hidden power or powers behind these supernatural abilities, I didn't ask questions, or pursue them in any way, and the buzzing disappeared.

Around this same time, while chatting with a friend, I was asked the question, "What's your goal in life?" What popped out of my mouth, much to my surprise and her bewilderment was, "I want to know God." She responded by saying, "Don't you want something more material, like a nice house or a new car?" And I responded, "That's not it for me!"

When I thought about my answer, I realized what had occurred in my subconscious. Because I had witnessed indisputable evidence of the supernatural realm in creation and also in the spiritists' practices, in my mind, I had deemed it best to get to know, "Number One." But, not knowing how to accomplish this goal, I just continued my spiritual explorations as I felt led.

The last experience with Eastern thought was my participation in the program at the Living Love Center run by Ken Keyes, Jr. This center taught a western adaptation of Buddhist principles. The main premise of the center was, if you are not attached to any worldly desires, then you can live lovingly and at peace with yourself and others.

We were given ten principles to meditate upon daily, which were to assist you in staying free from the security, sensation and power addictions that bound you. Additionally, every morning, a group meeting took place. At the meeting, each person was to talk about something that had aroused their anger the day before, a sure sign of attachment, and which principle they had applied in the situation, or the one or ones that should have been applied. The others in the group offered suggestions too.

But after a short stay at the center, I began to feel restless again. I had been living in densely populated areas, and had been exposed to so many new ideas in a brief time, that I felt I needed to go where there was more open space to free my mind and gain some peace. But I didn't know anyone who owned land in the country. Consequently, I decided to go back to school to get my California teaching credential, and I chose the most remote school in the University of California system, which was Humboldt State University in Arcata, California, 90 miles south of the Oregon border.

COMING INTO THE LIGHT

> "When Jesus spoke again to the people, he said,
> 'I am the light of the world. Whoever follows me will
> never walk in darkness, but will have the light of life.'"
> (John 8:12 NIV)

I was accepted at Humboldt State, as a graduate student in the Education Department.

Just before leaving Berkeley, I went to visit the spiritist I had been seeing. Without me mentioning my plans, she told me I was leaving the Bay Area that I would once again be a classroom teacher, and her most perplexing statement was that, I would acquire the "highest form of spiritual knowledge." I had no idea what she meant by that, and I figured if she knew what it was, she would have this knowledge herself.

So I tucked away that bit of information, got a ride north to Arcata, and moved into the only hotel in town. In a few weeks, after getting settled, I walked to campus with one thing in mind—find a work/study job.

In the Sociology Department, I interviewed for a research assistant's position that involved working for two professors, who wanted to compare the teaching strategies used in a Christian school, with those in the public schools. As a former public school teacher and someone interested in spiritual ideas, they thought I was a suitable candidate for the job, which entailed observing classes being taught at the new Christian school run by the First Baptist Church of Arcata. Was this God's way of leading a seeking soul to the truth?

One of the professors working on the project was a Christian who attended the First Baptist Church. After my interview, Professor Anderson and I talked for a while, and he invited me to a prayer meeting being held that evening. Out of curiosity, I decided to go to the meeting to see what the "Christians" were all about. At the time, I was not willing to reject any spiritual path.

That evening at the prayer meeting, made up mostly of students, several people related to me the biblical explanation of who Jesus was, and what He had come to do.

I, however, could not agree with what they were saying. Having done some reading about the more mystical nature of the "Christ Consciousness," which I had learned was a spiritual "state of mind" seeking to be pure and in harmony with God and everything in the cosmos, I couldn't accept the idea of an actual person being "the Christ."

They didn't give up on me, and sent out another lifeline. After praying for me, I was invited to attend the Sunday morning worship service at the First Baptist Church.

When Sunday morning arrived, I felt compelled to attend that service. Little did I know that my presence there that morning, would become the turning point of my life.

I arrived at church a little after the service had begun and stood in the vestibule listening to the singing and watching the worshippers. I was moved by the sense of reverence that filled the sanctuary, as I witnessed the congregation lifting up their voices and hands in worship to God.

Then three sentiments came to my mind. The first two were: "What's a nice Jewish girl from Brooklyn doing in a place like this with these straight, redneck people?" (These protests represented first my Jewish, and then my antiestablishment views). The third insight, which overshadowed the first two objections was: "These people know the God whom they are worshipping, and I want that, too." As I was pondering these thoughts, a still small voice whispered in my mind, "This is the truth," and I knew at that moment, my spiritual quest was over.

Unlike my experience with TM and Spiritism, which aroused fear of the unknown, the beauty and sincerity of the worship I had just witnessed, helped me decide, that what these Christians had was something worth pursuing. I had finally found the gateway to knowing God. It was through Jesus. The Bible states it this way: "Enter through the narrow gate. For wide is the gate and broad is the road that leads to destruction, and many enter through it. But small is the gate and narrow the road that leads to life..." (Matthew 7:13-14 NIV).

GROWING IN KNOWLEDGE

"But grow in the grace and knowledge
of our Lord and Savior Jesus Christ."
(2 Peter 3:18 NKJV)

In the fall of 1973, I started attending Sunday morning services at the First Baptist Church of Arcata.

Now that I was a believer, I was satisfied in my spirit that I had come into a relationship with God through Jesus. But, I did have a problem. During the services, I would get knots in my stomach when I heard Jesus's name. It was a reflex action caused by the negative associations to His name, that I had acquired growing up Jewish. In time, however, those physical responses began to fade.

Also at that time, while still living at the hotel, I began talking with some of the residents about Christianity, with the hope of gaining some knowledge about it from them. They, however, were either into New Age philosophies, or had been exposed to Christianity growing up, but were not interested in practicing the faith now.

I soon came to the conclusion that I should live among other Christians in order to grow in understanding, and gain support for my newfound faith.

One day after the semester had begun, I went to class and found that it had been cancelled. I walked up the block to the First Baptist Church to see if anyone there could help me find a suitable place to live. At the church I met the assistant pastor and asked him if he knew of any people who were interested in having a Christian student live with them. "As it happened," a young man was there who heard my request, and said he thought his parents were looking for students to move in with them, since he and his sister had moved to a Christian farm, and his brother had left to get married.

Thus, I called the Grytnesses. They were indeed opening their home up to Christian students.

The next day I arrived at the Grytness home and met with Mr. Grytness. After a short conversation, he asked me this question: "If you were to die tomorrow and St. Peter met you at Heaven's door and asked, 'Why should you be allowed to enter Heaven?' What would be your answer?"

My response was, "Because Jesus died for my sins." I had become a believer in the sacrificial, atoning death of Jesus for the sins of humanity, including my own. I was forgiven. My transgressions would no longer keep me apart from God, both in this life, and for eternity.

Mr. Grytness replied, "You're in!"

Shortly, thereafter, I moved into the Grytness home, where there were two empty bedrooms with double-decker beds. I was their first live-in student and a brand new baby Christian!

The Grytnesses, Dale and Joy, were warm, caring people, who were always available to answer my questions.

Looking back I remember, as a new believer, sitting in their living room trying to read through the New Testament as if it were a novel. I was hungry to know the word of God, and to grow in my understanding of God's ways. I was practicing what the apostle Peter encouraged when he wrote, "Like newborn babies, crave pure spiritual milk, so that by it you may grow up in your salvation, now that you have tasted that the Lord is good" (1 Peter 2:2-3 NIV).

I hadn't been with the Grytnesses for very long, when a unique experience occurred. It happened one afternoon as I was walking home from school through the town's Redwood Forest. (Arcata, being near the coast, is in the midst of Northern California's Redwood country).

It was a quiet overcast day. I walked along the road that cut through the forest, and came out onto the part of the road that skirted a large open field. Unexpectedly, I began thinking about all the wrong things I had done in my life. A deep sense of grief for these transgressions came over me. I felt terrible.

When I got home, I told Joy about my experience. Her reaction surprised me. She was actually glad for me. She told me I was experiencing the conviction of the Holy Spirit for my sins. This was very good because if I didn't know how grievous my sins were in God's eyes, I wouldn't know how desperately I needed the Savior who willingly paid the penalty for them. I didn't comprehend all she said at the time, but Joy's explanation provided some comfort, and insight into the work of the Holy Spirit.

Some days later, I took it upon myself to perform a symbolic gesture which to me marked my entry into a new life. This token act involved the disposal of a pair of blue jeans I had worn for a long time. I had considered these jeans, with embroidery down the legs, a work of art. Their most notable feature, however, were its colorful patches. There were patches on top of patches! When I thought about those jeans, I realized they represented what I had been trying to do with my life. My various attempts at patching up the holes in my life through politics, and Eastern Philosophy hadn't worked very well either. I had needed something brand new. The Bible describes life as a believer this way: "If anyone is in Christ, he is a new creation; old things have passed away; behold, all things have become new" (2 Corinthians 5:17 *NKJV*).

This newness of life was evidenced by the continuing work of the Holy Spirit, the third person of the triune Godhead, in my heart.

Through the years of my radical political activities, I had become alienated from the mainstream of American life, and developed hostility towards my country, and its capitalistic system. I even distanced myself from my family (over 3,000 miles), who I viewed as part of the "Establishment."

But through the Spirit, I began to change on the inside. At one point, I sensed a breaking within me which I realized was God fulfilling his promise in Ezekiel 11:19, "I will remove from their bodies the hearts of stone and give them hearts of flesh" (Complete Jewish Bible). This change of heart led to a new way of thinking. I began to acknowledge that the system of government wasn't at fault in America; instead, it was the sin nature of people, which caused them to make selfish and greedy decisions. Then, I actually began to appreciate our country for the ideals of freedom and justice upon which the founding fathers had established our nation; and for the hope of a good life one may have through our democratic process and free enterprise system.

Finally, God restored love in my heart for my family; and He gave me the ability to want to accept and forgive their shortcomings. Now that I'd been forgiven my errors, it was easier to learn to forgive others theirs.

Another change that was taking place was that living with the Grytnesses provided a more structured lifestyle than what I had been experiencing. In addition to my graduate school courses, I was now attending services every Sunday morning and evening, and a Bible study held in their home Wednesday evenings.

Since Mr. Grytness was one of eight elders in the church, he held weekly Bible study/prayer meetings in his home, with several families and students who lived nearby. These meetings were an attempt to make church life more personal, and also to help with any need that may arise within the group. I was also assigned a young woman from the church who instructed me on some basic doctrines of the faith. As far as being discipled by the Grytnesses, themselves, it wasn't done so much by what they said, but how they lived.

For instance, they encouraged reading God's word, by having weekly Bible studies and going to Sunday School. They demonstrated the value of family, by occasionally having family get-togethers with their kids, where there were sing-alongs and popcorn. And finally, they demonstrated a zeal for serving God, in whatever ways He led (like opening their doors to Christian students)!

So, given my environment, I was growing in faith, knowledge of God's Word, and discipline. However, there was one concept I didn't as yet grasp.

When I first attended the church and people heard I was a Jew, they would embrace me and say, "Now you're a completed Jew." But, I had no idea what they meant. Having only one or two Jewish believers in their congregation, the members didn't have the experience in explaining the Jewish aspects of Christianity. It took me two years to learn about, The Jewish Connection!

The One

O, can it be?
HaShem has heard our plea
And sent His only
      begotten Son
To deliver us from
      the cruel
           taskmaster, Satan.

Bless HaShem,
      for Meshiach has come—
Not, as yet, in flowing robes
      to rule and reign,
But as a Servant Redeemer,
      to give His all
That we could know
      His great love—
He, who came from above,
To be the Atoning One.

Bless HaShem,
      O my soul,
For He has set me free
From sin's strangle hold.
Now I rejoice and sing
And praise my one
      and only King.

Yeshua, my Deliverer,
      will one day return,
To take His place
      on David's throne.
Then all men will know
      the excellence of Him—
The True and Righteous One.

JESUS IS JEWISH

"Are you the *Mashiach*,...?"
(Mark 14:61 Complete Jewish Bible)

While browsing in a Christian book store, I came across two biographies by Jewish believers like myself one was <u>Ben Israel</u> by Arthur Katz, the other was <u>Michael, Michael Why Do You Hate Me?</u> by Michael Esses. I purchased the books, took them home and devoured them.

When reading Ben Israel, I was moved by Mr. Katz's tenacious international search for the purpose of life, which he discovered was serving God, through the Messiah Jesus. Then in Michael Esses' book, I was amazed how the Messiah Jesus finally got this Orthodox Jewish man's attention. Thus, it was through reading about their encounters with God, and how they came to understand that Jesus is the prophesied Messiah[*][†], that I too accepted this truth.

What a difference it made to me to learn that the Hebrew rendering of Christ is *Meshiach*. While growing up, I had always heard that a person who "converted" to Christianity was no longer a Jew. This person had abandoned his people, and was considered a traitor. But, now I learned that I did not give up my birthright. I was still a Jew and Jesus is Jewish too. This knowledge gave me a tremendous sense of relief.

---

[*] For the name Jesus (Greek) means "God Saves," the Hebrew is Yeshua. Christ (Greek) means "The Anointed One," the Hebrew being *Meshiach*. Thus, Jesus Christ (Greek) and *Yeshua Hameshiach* (Hebrew) mean, "God saves through the Anointed One."

[†] Appendix pp. 67-69 for Messianic prophesies.

Hence, I came to understand that I did not convert from one religion to another, but I did *t'suvah* (Hebrew), "a turning," (that is, repentance) from sin to God; all made possible by faith in the atoning work of Yeshua, the Messiah. Now my sins no longer separated me from God as the prophet Isaiah declares is Israel's condition in Chapter 59:2.*

After making the discovery that Jesus is the Messiah, and reclaiming my Jewish identity, the Lord began to fill my heart with love for my Jewish brethren and a love for the Jewish homeland, Eretz Yisroel, the land of Israel.

Then because of this love for my people, and as a testimony that I haven't forsaken them, I prayed: "Lord, if I am to marry, let it be to another Jewish believer or a Gentile believer with a heart for the Jews."

Soon after gaining my new understanding of the Jewishness of the New Covenant established by the Jewish Messiah, an opportunity arose at school to express my interest in Jewish affairs. This occurred when one of my political science professors allowed me to do an independent study on the biblical basis of the Arab-Israeli conflict and what the Bible says will be its conclusion.

Through doing the research and then writing the paper (which was well received by my professor), my love for Israel intensified so much so, that I decided I wanted to make *alliyah* that is, "to go up" to the Jewish homeland, Israel, and become a citizen. Something had happened in the seven years since returning from Israel to bring about a change of heart and mind toward Israel. That something was God!

Consequently, I made a phone call and had an initial interview with an Israeli official in San Francisco, which went well. The door appeared to be opened for me to go and become a teacher in Israel.

A week or two later, I received an official application for Israeli citizenship.

While filling out the application, I found one item that was troublesome to me—the line read, Religion. I was perplexed about what to write. I thought of myself as being Jewish, loving the God of my Fathers, and the prophesied Messiah whom He sent. But, I wanted to make sure I did the

---

* Appendix p. 73

right thing. So, I went to see Pastor Jackson of the First Baptist Church and asked his advice about what to write.

I told him how I viewed myself. But he said I needed to make my beliefs clear, because then I would know for sure if it was God's will that I go. He continued, "If it was God's will, whatever I wrote wouldn't make a difference, because He could even make the person reading the application skip over that line." So, I wrote, Hebrew Christian, a term that is used at times to connote Jewish believers in Yeshua.

Within a couple of weeks, I received a letter stating my application for Israeli citizenship was rejected. Apparently, my desire to go to Israel to defend, pray for and support its statehood, though a heartfelt cause, was not God's will for me.

Thus, I had my first major test in following Messiah's ways, in this case, telling the truth no matter the consequences. Since He had become my Lord and Shepherd, I was now dedicated to following His commandments and His lead.

Miryam's Song

Miryam: What a bright light.
                Who can this be?

Gabriel: Myriam, you have found
                favor with God,
                      my dear,
                You need not fear.

Miryam: What words are these?
                The God who
                      sees,
                          knows,
                              remembers
                                    and cares
                Has spoken to me in my lowly estate!

Gabriel: You will bring forth
                    a son,
                And he will be called
                      The Righteous One.

Miryam: How can this be?
                I have known no man.

Gabriel: The Ruach Hakodesh
                    upon you will come.
                Thus the child will be
                    God's own Son.

Miryam: I am honored to be chosen.
Let it be to this handmaiden
As you have spoken.

"Abba, Father,
    I do magnify your Name,
    for You alone are holy.
Help me endure the shame caused by others.
Help dear Yoseph understand
    that I am his alone
    and have not known another."

"And together we will rejoice
    in this great thing
    You will do,

Bringing to pass
    the release of your people, Israel,
    from all sin,
        grief,
            sorrow,
                regret,
    from all that holds them fast."

RETURN HOME

"Trust in the Lord with all thy heart,
and lean not upon thine own understanding.
In all thy ways acknowledge Him, and He will direct thy paths."
(Proverbs 3:5-6 The Masoretic Text)

It was 1977. I had not only received my California teaching credential, but, in addition, after taking a few extra courses, I had also completed the requirements for a Master's in Education. Thus, my schooling in California had concluded. And since I was not going to Israel, I decided to go back east to visit my family.

It was summertime, and there was no better place to be than Rockaway Beach. My parents lived in an apartment building across the street from the boardwalk that ran along the beach and coastal waters of the Atlantic Ocean.

After finishing several years of graduate school, I was content to relax in the sun and surf, and reconnect with my family. A dear aunt of mine was not well that summer, so I had plenty of time to visit with her too.

Then, as the summer was coming to an end, I was feeling unsure about what I was supposed to do next. I realized it was time to pray for guidance. Consequently, early one morning I took my Bible to the boardwalk, sat on the steps that led down to the beach and asked God to reveal His will for the next chapter in my life.

Was I to go back to California or stay in Rockaway? As I read through the Scriptures, it became clear to me that it was time to stay in New York and strengthen family ties. In Ecclesiastes 3:1 it states, "There is a time for everything, and a season for every activity under heaven." Then in verse 7 it says there's, "a time to tear and a time to mend" (NIV). After being apart from my family for ten years, it was time to bind together again.

When I had reclaimed my Jewish identity, I knew that I would eventually leave Arcata to live in a metropolitan area where there was a large Jewish population, among whom I'd bear witness about Yeshua. But I didn't think it would be back in my hometown!

Now that I had decided to stay in Rockaway, it was time to deal with the basics—a job, a new place to fellowship, and a place to live. Living in my parents one-bedroom apartment was not a long term option.

For the next few years, while living in Rockaway, I began working in the field that would eventually become my career.

Because my New York City Elementary School Teaching License had lapsed, I could not teach for the Board of Education. The jobs I did acquire were as an after-school counselor for multi-handicapped children, who resided in group homes or larger residences.

Eventually, in two instances my job description changed. At the first job, through a grant that was awarded to the residence, I began teaching fine and gross motor skills to children in the after-school program. In the second instance, under the direction of my group home's psychologist, I began applying interpersonal therapy to individual, severely autistic children.

While I enjoyed the challenges of working with these special needs children, the private agencies I worked for had difficulties sustaining the funding for their programs. Thus, I moved from one job to the next in a few years.

The second aspect of my life that was important to me was, to find a suitable place of worship. As a believer in the Messiah Yeshua, I needed to attend a place where it was taught that Jesus was the Redeemer of Israel, as well as, the nations.

Having grown up in Rockaway, I knew of all the synagogues in town, but not the churches. To help solve my problem, I called the 700 Club, a Christian television broadcast, and asked if they could recommend a church in my area. They directed me to a small, but vibrant congregation, where I became a member for the next fifteen years and also came under the wings of another wonderful couple, Carmen and Jenny Maffei.

LOVE AND MARRIAGE

"But seek first the Kingdom of God and His righteousness,
and all these things shall be added to you."
(Matthew 6:33 *NKJV*)

My life in New York had settled into a routine. I was working steadily and attending worship services and other fellowship activities regularly. Then one day while waiting on line at the Post Office, I saw a fellow who was holding a magazine published by a Messianic Jewish organization. I was curious, and began to ask him questions about the magazine.

This young man and I talked for a while. Subsequently, I found out that he had gone to my high school, graduating a year before me, and that he too was a Jewish believer in Jesus. Interestingly, he was also single!

Ding! Ding! The bells were going off in my mind. Could this young man be the answer to the prayer I had made five years before in Arcata? Could he be the one??!

Soon after our meeting, I invited Greg to attend a worship service with me. Then, we began to see each other regularly. Every Sunday, he would pick me up and we'd go to church together.

However, after a couple of months, I sensed that Greg was going to church to be with me, rather than to worship God. Finally, it reached the point where I knew I needed to mention something to him. Thus, after service one Sunday, I told Greg that I felt it wasn't the right time for a relationship between us, because he first had to make sure his relationship with God was where it should be.

After saying what I did, I was still hoping Greg would come to church. I even had some of the men call him and invite him out. But he never came back, and we never saw each other again.

Initially, I was disappointed. Greg fit the main qualification for a potential husband—he was a Jewish believer. But, after the Holy Spirit whispered to me, "You'd be bored", when thinking about a long term relationship with him, I knew that the exhortation which states, "Do not be unequally yoked" (2 Corinthians 6:14 *NKJV*) when considering a marriage partner, applied in a wider range than to just unbelievers.

This situation was yet another test in my relationship with the Lord. I had put pleasing God ahead of even my desire to get married. Thus, while I didn't have a ring, I had His peace and knew, therefore, that I had made the right choice.

A year later another young man, who was also Jewish, started coming to church. He had been visiting on and off, but by the end of 1980, Jeff had determined to follow God's ways and was coming regularly to services.

At first, I was physically attracted to Jeffrey. However, I prayed about that, because I knew there would have to be more than a physical attraction to form a meaningful relationship with anyone. Then, as the weeks went by, and we had the opportunity to interact during church activities, my feelings for him got stronger. As I began to get breathless and have knots in my stomach when I saw him, I knew it was time to pray seriously about Jeffrey and not just by myself; I also asked a few of my friends to pray with me about this possible match.

Finally, I reached the point when I couldn't go on without knowing where I stood; so I approached Jeff and admitted I had feelings for him, and asked if he had any feelings towards me. I was desperate. I had to know if these feelings were of God, or if my own desires were getting the best of me. I am not sure what Jeff thought about my boldness, but he said calmly that, no, he didn't have special feelings for me, but he would pray about it too. Later, I found out, he had been looking around among the single women in the church for he wanted a wife!

At first, Jeff was reluctant to think about me as a possible mate, because I was a good deal older than him. But, God, must have intervened for he started to call me, and we would have long chats on the phone.

Then one Saturday afternoon, some weeks later, Jeff called and told me he was no longer coming to our church. He had decided to attend a different ministry, which met on Saturday evenings, and he was planning to go that night.

I was disappointed at first, thinking I might not see Jeffrey again. But, then I pondered two possibilities. The first was, perhaps, there was something new Jeff would learn, and then he would come back and teach it to me; or, he just wasn't the one for me and he'd be gone for good.

In my mind, I released the situation to God. I was willing to put Jeffrey on the altar, and let God again have His perfect will in my life. As Abraham was willing to put his beloved son, Isaac, on the altar of sacrifice, to demonstrate his love and trust in God, I also surrendered my own desires to God. Again, God gave me His peace "which surpasses all understanding" (Philippians 4:7 *NKJV*).

The next day, much to my surprise, Jeffrey, looking a bit sheepish, was at the morning service. When he saw me, he asked if we could talk after the service.

Later, back at my home, Jeff explained that he had made a mistake about this other ministry; it wasn't what he had expected. Then the conversation drifted to more personal matters. Finally, Jeffrey declared, that he knew I was the one for him. What a difference twenty four hours made! After I had surrendered my love to God, he was given back to me with a bonus—a proposal!

In the following months, Jeffrey and I saw a lot of each other. Often on his way home from work, he would come by my job just to say hello. We also visited with each other's parents several times. Then in a short time, we started to make wedding plans.

When I spoke to my parents initially, they were not pleased that I wanted to marry another believer in Messiah Jesus. It was upsetting to me having a conflict with them when I was so happy. But the Lord led me to a verse that was comforting: "When my father and my mother forsake me, Then the Lord will take care of me" (Psalms 27:10 NKJV). Later, He assured me: "The blessing of the Lord makes one rich, and He adds no sorrow with it" (Proverbs 10:22 *NKJV*).

In light of our parents' feelings (Jeff's parents were not pleased with his new beliefs either), Jeff and I wanted to demonstrate to them, through our wedding ceremony, that we still considered ourselves Jewish.

The first minister we contacted to do the service was from the Jews for Jesus organization; but that connection did not work out.

After a premarital interview the Rabbi from the temple where I had grown up agreed to marry us, even though he did not approve of our beliefs. We also decided to have a second ceremony conducted by a minister who shared our beliefs.

Consequently, on June 11, 1981, at West End Temple, Jeffrey and I took our first wedding vows. It was a small ceremony with only our parents, and Jeff's sister as the maid of honor, and his brother-in-law as the best man. Then, three days later, on June 14, our pastor from Full Gospel Tabernacle, Robert Castro, married us again at the Rockaway Park American Legion Hall. At this wedding, our family and all our friends, including my spiritual mentors, the Grytnesses, were in attendance to help us celebrate our entrance into the blessings of the covenant relationship of marriage.

Thus, the two ceremonies reflected our connection to both our historical Jewish roots, as well as, our acceptance of the New Covenant God had established with us, through the Messiah Yeshua.

Through the two romantic relationships in which I was involved, God had shown me that He wants us to trust Him with all the decisions in our lives, especially the ones that are the most important to us. For He is a loving Heavenly Father whose desire is to bless His children. In Jeremiah 29:11 He says, "I know the plans I have for you... plans to prosper you and not to harm you, plans to give you hope and a future"(NIV). Later, Yeshua stated, "I have come so that they may have life, life in its fullest measure" (John 10:10 Complete Jewish Bible).

THE CHILDREN

"He causes the childless woman to live
at home happily as a mother of children."
(Psalm 113:9 Complete Jewish Bible)

Having married in my mid-thirties, both Jeff and I felt the urgency to start a family, and within two months I was pregnant.

As the months of my pregnancy passed, I began to feel intimidated by the prospect of giving birth. Therefore, I hung the following verse, written in large letters, on my bedroom wall: "God is our refuge and strength, a very present help in trouble, therefore, we will not fear" (Psalm 46:1-2a *NKJV*). I meditated on this verse daily and was greatly encouraged by its promises.

And except for the first couple of months of morning sickness, my pregnancy went along without any problems.

When I was nearing my due date, Jeff and I went to the La Maze classes, to prepare for the natural childbirth method of delivery.

Finally, the day arrived. Jeff blazed a trail from Rockaway to the Caledonian Hospital in Brooklyn. We had to travel to Brooklyn, about a forty-five minute trip, because our doctor, the one who had delivered Jeffrey twenty-six years earlier, was affiliated with that hospital.

When at last we arrived safely, with me practicing the La Maze breathing techniques throughout the length of the car ride, I was settled in a room on the maternity floor.

Then after a couple of hours of regular sets of contractions, the time had come for me to go into the delivery room, accompanied by my faithful La Maze coach, Jeffrey.

I wasn't in the delivery room for very long, before the doctor told me it was time to start pushing. Thus, when the contractions occurred, I pushed; but, nothing happened. After a succession of contractions and pushes, without the baby descending, the atmosphere in the room, began to become a bit tense. My dear husband was getting nervous, as was the doctor who feared that the baby's life may be in jeopardy.

Finally, the doctor made the decision to use forceps, and I was given a local anesthetic in my lower back. From that point on, the delivery went quickly, and within minutes, a beautiful baby girl was born. I remember holding my daughter, a pink cherub with a shock of dark hair, and experiencing one of the most joyous moments of my life.

Later as I reflected upon the delivery, I realized that while Sarah's birth was very trying, I had peace throughout the experience. For meditating on the word of God had given me the assurance, that God would keep me and my baby from harm. Similarly, during the birth, God was reassuring Jeffrey of His divine presence with the verse: "Can a woman forget her suckling child, that she should not have compassion on the son of her womb? Yea, these may forget, Yet will I not forget thee" (Isaiah 49:15 The Masoretic Text).

The birth of our son, Jonathan, two years later went more smoothly; but God, showed his faithfulness in that situation, too.

At the time of this pregnancy, my in-laws had no other grandchildren but our daughter, Sarah. Knowing my father-in law was an active guy, I felt that he would appreciate having a grandson to one day do the outdoorsy things grandpas and grandsons like to do together. So I prayed, and asked God for a son, as a way of blessing Grandpa Ralph.

On the morning of Jonathan's birth, Jeff "happened" to be reading the passage in the New Covenant which include these verses: "Now Elizabeth's *(my name)* full time came for her to be delivered and she brought forth a son... and his mother answered and said... he shall be called John"(Luke 1:57, 60 NKJV italics mine).

So when our son was born by natural childbirth, thankfully, without incident, Jeff said we should call him John, according to the Scripture he had read that day.

Coincidentally, prior to his birth, I had been considering boys names that started with the letter, "J", in remembrance of both our grandmothers, Yetta (in Hebrew the letter J is substituted with the letter Y) and Jenny.

So when Jeff mentioned the name, John, I recalled liking the name, Jonathan, and suggested that instead. Jeff liked it, too. Later, I looked up its meaning, and found that it meant in Hebrew, "Gift of God" or "Jehovah has given."

Thus, our precious son, Jonathan, was given by God in direct answer to a mother's prayer, whose intention was to especially bless the *zaida* (Yiddish, grandpa).

FIRES AND FLOODS

"When you pass through the waters, I will be with you;
and through the rivers they shall not overflow you.
When you walk through the fire, you shall not
be burned, nor shall the flame scorch you."
(Isaiah 43:2 NKJV)

Many families go through adversities. In the earliest years of our marriage, we experienced trouble mainly from two sources—water and fire.

When Jeff and I got married, we moved into the ground floor of a three-family house in Rockaway. In the beginning, things were fine and cozy in our one bedroom apartment. But one stormy day, adversity came right to our door.

Our apartment ran alongside the driveway of the house. On this particular day, when it had rained hard and long, the rainwater found the lowest point in the driveway. It was a dip in the center. That dip, acted like a funnel, as it channeled water right under our front door and into the apartment. We were soon walking in four inches of water. It happened so quickly and unexpectedly, that we lost carpeting and things that were on the floor in our closets. When the water had finally receded, we were relieved and felt glad the damage had not been worse.

Thankfully, some work was done on the driveway, and water no longer found its way under our front door. However, trial by water in that apartment was not, as yet, over.

While cleaning up in the kitchen one evening, I heard some water running in the room above me. I didn't think much about it, and walked out of the kitchen when I had finished my chores. Shortly thereafter, however, I heard a loud crash coming from the kitchen. When I hurried back, I saw that our dropped ceiling had collapsed, and water was cascading down from the bathroom above. Apparently, one of the children from upstairs had left the water running in the tub. The water overflowed and became too heavy for our ceiling and down it came. Again, we had a mess to clean up, but we were fortunate no one had gotten hurt.

After a few years in that apartment, having survived the watery mishaps, our family had grown from two to four people. We needed more space. We decided to buy a house, and purchased a three-family residence in Rockaway, to give us additional income. It was in this house that the last water episode of note occurred. It happened during the Nor'easter of November 1992.

On that day, it had begun raining in the morning. As the rain continued to fall, the water level in the street rose. In the early afternoon, Jeff waded out to his van and was able to drive it away to higher ground.

By about two o'clock, I noticed the water outside was so high, that it had covered the fire hydrant in front of the house next door.

I wasn't too concerned about water coming into our home, since there was a staircase from the street to the porch outside our door. I did notice, however, that due to the depth of the water, Jeff would be unable to return home; and I was curious about what had happened to him. I didn't have to wonder too long, because shortly thereafter, there was a knock on our door. When I opened it, I saw a police officer in hip-high waders, and he informed me that my husband had sent him to evacuate my son and me!

After grabbing our coats, Jonathan and I cautiously got into a rubber raft, and were pulled two blocks, through 3 1/2 feet of water to higher ground, passing floating cars, along the way.

When we got to Beach Channel Drive, we found Jeff there with his van. We waited a little longer for Sarah, who was let out of school through the playground, onto Beach Channel Drive. Then the four of us huddled into the van filled with auto parts, and went to stay at grandma's house, a twelve-story apartment building, in Rockaway.

Since our basement was flooded, we lost our heat, hot water and electricity, making it necessary for us to stay with my parents for a few days, until our utilities were restored.

During that time, Jeff made several trips back to the house to pump the water out of the basement. Then with the help of a neighbor, he was able to get the utilities going again, and we were finally able to return home.

Thus, the waters came and went. In their wake, we lost such things as carpeting, a water heater, an oil burner, and the dearest loss to me, was a small group of wedding pictures that could not be replaced. But, thankfully, by God's grace, we were all kept safe.

However, during the years of living in this three-family house, we also experienced trials by fire.

The first occurred, when our tenant on the second floor fell asleep while smoking in bed, and set her mattress on fire.

The fire department was called and they promptly threw the burning mattress out the bedroom window, keeping the fire from spreading. Fortunately, our neighbor was not hurt and the only damage, other than to her mattress, was a charred floor and broken windows throughout the second floor.

Our family was not home at the time of the fire. What a shock it was to return home to that mess. However, we were very glad the fire had been contained, and that no one had been injured.

The last fire occurred one summer night, while we were all sleeping.

At two o'clock in the morning, one of our neighbors banged on our front door to wake us up. He quickly explained that the house next door, which had been undergoing renovations, was on fire, and we needed to evacuate our home immediately, in case the fire should spread.

We hurriedly gathered Sarah and Jonathan still in their pajamas, and placed them in our car in the driveway, on the other side of the house away from the burning building.

Then Jeff and I along with some neighbors stationed ourselves in front of our house to watch the firefighters do their gallant work.

Sometime before the blaze was brought under control, we noticed the flames from the burning dwelling beginning to lap the side of our house, causing the tar under the shingles to drip down the siding. It was a fearsome sight.

Finally, however, after several hours, the firefighters declared that the fire was completely out. There had been no further damage to our property.

Thus, while these trials created stress, some property loss and, at times, disruption in our usual life routines, we were grateful that God had kept us from injury, therefore, fulfilling his prophesy from Isaiah 43:2.

BACK TO TEACHING

"The steps of a good man are ordered by the Lord."
(Psalm 37:23 NKJV)

When the children were old enough to help out with some chores, Jeff and I decided that it was time, and financially essential, for me to go back to work. Therefore, in the early 1990s, I began to substitute teach in several of the local elementary schools.

I hadn't worked in a school for ten years, and I was curious to see the changes that had taken place during those years. I was pleasantly surprised, when I noticed in a few instances, classrooms with libraries containing shelves filled with excellent children's books. In addition, on display were reports, stories and art projects that expressed the children's responses to the literature they had read. I inquired about this form of teaching that had children respond to literature in diverse ways, and found out it was called, Whole Language Education.

I was so impressed by the quality of the work the teachers were drawing from the children that I decided to take some courses to learn what I could about this new method of teaching.

Through my inquiries, I learned that one of the local universities had a fifteen credit program leading to a certificate in Whole Language Education. I enrolled, thinking these courses would be a good preparation for me, before returning to teaching full time.

As I studied the different whole language strategies, I reminisced about the style of teaching in years passed, and how I had longed at the time, for a program that would have had a greater impact on my students. Now, I was gaining the means to better motivate and engage children in learning.

One of the main ideas of the whole language method, is to incorporate subject areas, such as, science, math and language studies around a central theme. This integrated approach, helps children to appreciate and make more sense of the world in which they live.

Thus, on the days when I wasn't substituting, I would be preparing charts of poems and songs, coordinating them with picture books, relevant to different themes that I could use in the early-childhood classes to which I had asked to be assigned. I also made up photo copies of games and puzzles to stimulate further language growth.

Then one day, as I was making copies in a local store, I met a teacher who influenced me to take yet another turn in the course of my teaching career.

SPECIAL EDUCATION

"My grace is sufficient for you,
for My strength is made perfect in weakness."
(2 Corinthians 12:9a *NKJV*)

While Ms. Meehan and I were chatting and making our copies, I mentioned to her that I was a substitute teacher in Rockaway. When she heard this news she seemed delighted. She went on to explain that the special education school in which she taught was located on the top floor of a private religious school. And because of its unusual location, substitute teachers were unaware of the school's existence. She, therefore, invited me to visit the building in order to see if I would be interested in substituting there.

Shortly after our conversation, I called the school and made arrangements for a tour of the site.

The visit was informative and encouraging. The staff seemed friendly, and the classes were, for the most part, orderly. In addition, I was glad to see several aides in each room to help individualize the program for the students, aged five to nine years old.

Consequently, before I left the building, I gave the secretary my telephone number, and let her know I was available anytime.

Thus, the outcome of my encounter with Ms. Meehan was, I became a regular substitute teacher at her school, and worked there 45 days that first year.

Additionally, after having success in motivating the students with my lessons, as well as, enjoying the team teaching approach within the classrooms, I decided to pursue certification in special education. I further reasoned—there always seemed to be a need for special education teachers.

Another incentive to getting an additional certification was, at the time, the New York City teacher's union, The United Federation of Teachers, was cosponsoring graduate courses in education with various universities at reduced cost. These afternoon and evening courses were held in public schools throughout the city, thus, allowing me to take courses in special education at locations near the Rockaway schools in which I was teaching. It was a great convenience. But, what amazed me most about this opportunity, however, was that as a substitute teacher I wasn't even a member of the United Federation of Teachers! I was, nevertheless, allowed to enroll in the program.

Therefore, within a couple of years of trying to balance work, studies, and family responsibilities, by the grace of God, I completed 28 graduate credits including student teaching, and earned my New York State Permanent Certificate in Special Education.

Over the next few years, I taught at several schools, until I found a special education program that was a good match. It was in an early childhood center that encouraged the teachers to create a stimulating curriculum for the students. They supported the teachers efforts with continuous staff development, including workshops and visits to various cultural locations. In addition, they offered excellent health benefits for their employees. Thus, I remained at that school for the next eight years.

Through the years, I found being a special education teacher a great challenge. Usually, the children I taught had multiple problems, especially in the areas of expressive and/or receptive language (not being able to understand or process the speech they were hearing); as well as, difficulties in social/emotional development. In addition, there was often some lag in fine and gross motor skills. Then inevitably, each year, there would be one or two children whose behavior was extreme in some way; either highly unmotivated or very aggressive and oppositional.

Consequently, the teaching practices involved much modeling, repetition, hands on experiences and patience. Fortunately, we had a support staff, which included teaching assistants, speech therapists, occupational therapists, psychologists and social workers who assisted in implementing the individualized treatment plans for the children.

The added benefit of this career was that it motivated me to draw closer to the Lord. Daily, I would cry out to Him for help and strength and all the qualities necessary including creativity, humor, meekness and wisdom, to be a cooperative colleague and an effective teacher for my students. So in retrospect, I thank God for putting me in an occupation that was beyond my natural abilities. It allowed me to experience the Lord's power working in me and to truly comprehend the verse, "My grace is sufficient for you, for My strength is made perfect in weakness" (2 Corinthians 12:9 NKJV).

CANCER

"Bless the Lord, Oh my soul; and all that is within me, bless His holy name! Bless the Lord, Oh my soul, and forget not all His benefits:... who heals all your diseases."
(Psalm 103:1-3 NKJV)

At the end of April 2002, I went for my annual pap smear. A few days later, I received the results which caused some anxiety. The findings revealed the presence of irregular cells. Consequently, I returned to my gynecologist for further testing. She performed two biopsies taking cells from both my uterus and cervix.

The results of the biopsies showed evidence of cancer cells in both places. Apparently, the cancer, which was at stage 3, was aggressive. It had originated in the uterus, then the endometrial cells had spread to the cervix.

This news was life altering. Instead of the usual thoughts of home, family and work, the predominant focus was now on dealing with cancer.

Upon the recommendation of my gynecologist, Jeff and I selected a gynecological oncologist. She, because of the aggressive nature of the cancer cells, strongly advised the surgical removal of my uterus.

Therefore, at the end of May 2002, I was admitted for surgery to Long Island Jewish Hospital, and was subsequently given a total hysterectomy. That is, as a precautionary measure, not only was my uterus removed, but my fallopian tubes and ovaries as well.

The results of the surgery were reported to us as positive, since the "wash" around the uterus was cancer free, as were several lymph nodes near the uterus that were also removed and tested.

Nevertheless, the protocol for treatment of uterine cancer included having a series of twenty six radiation treatments to the pelvic region, in order to combat any possible cancer cells that may have gone undetected.

Thus, after about a month of recuperation from surgery, I began going for radiation treatments, three times a week. Near the end of the radiation treatments, however, the radiation oncologist began to strongly recommend that I also get chemotherapy.

The reason for his insistence in this course of treatment was he had had a patient the year before with similar, aggressive stage 3 uterine cancer, who only had radiation treatments, and her cancer had returned within a year.

Since the protocol at the hospital limited follow-up treatment to radiation therapy (the doctors there were not satisfied with the extent of research done on drugs for uterine cancer at the time), Jeffrey and I had to make inquiries elsewhere in order to obtain chemotherapy.

Through some research with the American Cancer Society and contacts with other oncologists, we found out about trials taking place in New York City which were testing a drug to specifically combat uterine cancer. However, much to our dismay, I was too late to be part of the research as the trial period had already begun.

Nevertheless, since our radiation oncologist still felt strongly about getting chemo, he recommended a medical oncologist that he knew personally. When contacting her, however, we learned that she was not taking any new patients. But, before we totally lost hope, she directed us to another doctor who was able to treat me with the very same drug that was being used in the clinical trials.

Thus, a short time after I completed my radiation treatments, I began chemotherapy.

Over several fall months, I received four intravenous treatments of a cancer drug, as well as, anti-nausea medication. And, except for losing my hair, and being tired and achy the next day, the side effects were not substantial. Therefore, with the kind approval of my supervisor, knowing that once a month I would miss two consecutive days of work until the four treatments were complete, I was able to continue teaching during the fall of 2002.

Since that time, as the days, then years went by, and I have remained cancer free, Jeff and I have concluded, that I had been fortunate to have been given chemotherapy. And we have been grateful to God for leading us to a very caring and persistent radiation oncologist!

THE FALL

"...God causes everything to work together
for the good of those who love God and are
called in accordance with His purpose;..."
(Romans 8:28 Complete Jewish Bible)

On Sunday, January 25, 2009, while ice skating at our town's rink, the toe of my right skate got caught in a hole in the ice. Being unable to free my skate, I crashed to the ice and landed on my right side. After getting up slowly, I gingerly left the rink feeling a little achy.

That evening, the pain in my side increased substantially. Jeff took me to the emergency room at a nearby hospital where x-rays were taken. Although the x-rays did not reveal a fracture, I was advised to follow up with a visit to an orthopedic specialist.

Two days later, I visited with an orthopedic doctor, who took another x-ray, which again did not reveal a fracture. A couple of weeks later, however, when I was not improving, the orthopedist sent me for an MRI; which, showed a hairline fracture in the right ramus (a small pelvic bone.)

Thus, for several months, due to the pain from the fracture, my ability to move was limited. I had to stay home and rest, for I couldn't walk or sit for very long.

Then one day while I was lying in bed and praying, the Lord reminded me that I had been longing to see a current memoir written by a Messianic Jewish believer to share with my family. And He began to prompt me by putting in my mind the thought, "Since I couldn't get around very much, why don't I use the time to write my story."

Hope arose within me. Rather than languishing at home day after day, I could still be working to accomplish God's purposes, in this case, spreading knowledge to others of the Holy One of Israel, and His plan of reconciliation.

After putting several months in on this project, I began to realize that working full time with only six weeks' vacation would not have allowed the needed time and energy to complete a book. Then I wondered, did the Lord permit this accident to occur so that the recuperation time could be used to do this particular task?

I don't know the answer to that question. But, in the often lonely and painful year I've undergone while working on this memoir, I began rejoicing when thinking about the family members and friends who could be spiritually affected and enlightened when reading this work, and then I had to admit it, it was worth it all.

In addition, I was able to relate a bit better to the verse about Yeshua's suffering which states: "Who in exchange for obtaining the joy set before Him, *[returning to heaven knowing many will one day be with Him in glory]* endured execution on a stake as a criminal, scorning the shame" (Hebrews 12:2 Complete Jewish Bible; *italics are mine*).

RESTORATION

"And I will restore to you the
years that the locust hath eaten."
(Joel 2:25 The Masoretic Text)

In closing, I consider the above promise an explanation of what God has done in my life since being reconciled to Him through Messiah Yeshua. The following are some examples of what has occurred.

While in school, I had experienced difficulty learning due to a memory deficiency, which I believe I inherited from my father. When I had to study for an exam, I would cram enough information into my brain the night before, to usually enable me to pass the test. With the subjects in which I was particularly weak, I would have no qualms about cheating, since I felt the outside and inner pressures to excel were greater than the risk of getting caught. Thus, it was in this manner of cramming and cheating from my neighbor that I got through school.

As a believer, the Lord became my sufficiency. He spurred me on to better study skills, and directed me into courses that held my interest. Subsequently, when I returned to school in the 1990s to take the five course series in Whole Language Education, I received an A in each class and was invited to apply for membership in the Phi Beta Kappa honor society.

Then a more recent experience utilizing my memory has occurred, when I began studying an old paperback entitled, <u>French Through Pictures</u>. For almost a year, I've been working through the book and have learned much of what I couldn't absorb years ago. Needless to say, it had been a tremendous challenge for me to learn French in high school and college. What a delight it is now, with the help of the pictures, pronunciation guide and dictionary to finally make some headway in the language I had studied for so long.

Another activity I have enjoyed is dance, in particular, ballet. As a child I had taken ballet lessons, and then in later years, some modem dance classes. But as an adult, I had the desire to once again take ballet. However, it was difficult to find a beginners' adult class. I did, nevertheless, participate in two classes while living in Rockaway, but situations arose which brought my participation to an abrupt end.

Presently, however, I have found an excellent ballet teacher in the Adult Continuing Education program at our local Community College, and have taken her class for five semesters.

My motivation to endure the 1 1/2 hour class is to gain strength, flexibility and balance which are skills that require more effort to attain as one ages; plus, I enjoy the grace and beauty of ballet so much.

Finally, not only did I share these experiences to show how God transformed my life, but also as an answer to people who think that when a person begins to serve God, he has to forsake everything that he likes to do. I would say that my life with God demonstrates the opposite. For once God, through the Messiah, had forgiven my poor choices, He began to cleanse me from things that were harmful. Then He started to restore, and fulfill my heartfelt longings more than I could have imagined.

Amazing Love

What love is this
That the God of Avraham,
     Yitz'chak and Ya'akov
Would leave His glory,
Take on flesh, and dwell with us
In our sin-filled world.

To walk in our midst,
Teaching us the words of life,
Taking from us
     sickness and infirmities,
Giving us
     life and hope eternal.
Who, at the appointed time,
With tears and anguish,
Willingly went to the tree,
Where he was pierced
     hand
          foot
               side,
Paid for our crimes
Brought deliverance
From all that kept us confined.

And like Ya'akov, the supplanter,
Who wrestled with God for
     a night,
Gained new stature as Israel—
He who rules as God.

Yeshua, the Son of Man,
Wrestled with Satan three days
To rescue the souls of men,
Then rose in triumph—
    The Victorious Son of God!

What love is this?

The love of God for man.

AFTERWORD

Now that I've completed my testimony, I would like to share some of my observations after more than 40 years of embracing my Jewish heritage, and living by faith in the God of Abraham, Isaac and Jacob, and His Messiah.

First, I can say unwaveringly that the Old and New Covenants are the inspired word of God; that is, God revealing His message of love and reconciliation to people through His chosen prophets, and then through His Son.

Next, after being reconciled to God through the atoning work of Yeshua, the Messiah, one can have the experience of an intimate relationship with the living, loving, Almighty God by praying, reading the Bible as the Holy Spirit brings the Word to life, and by living according to its precepts.

After reading the Bible, you learn that the God of Abraham, Isaac and Jacob--the Creator--loves His creation, and mankind is at the top of His list. He demonstrated the enormity of His love towards us, when He became the atoning sacrifice for our sins.

Because we live in a fallen world (due initially to the choices of Adam and Eve in the garden; and then to the influence of the prince of this world, Satan), we will all go through problems and trials. However, when you are in a covenant relationship with God, He gives you comfort and strength, no matter what circumstances come your way.

In truth, I confess, coming from a family of worriers, the habit of worry (opposite of faith) has been recurrent. But, I've learned that the God of my fathers, and mothers Sarah, Rebekkah and Rachel is faithful to heal, bless and guide those who love and seek Him with all their heart.

Thus, I've written my story for this generation of Jewish and Gentile seekers, to let you know that Jesus (Yeshua) is the Jewish Messiah. He is also the Redeemer of all nations as the following Scripture testifies: "Indeed He says, 'It is too small a thing that You should be My Servant to raise up the tribes of Jacob, and to restore the preserved ones of Israel; I will also give You as a light to the Gentiles, that You should be My salvation to the ends of the earth'" (Isaiah 49:6 NKJV).

Two Women

(from the book of Ruth)

Naomi: HaShem, our life was good.
            You brought us out from the famine in Yisrael,
            And we lived in peace among the Gentiles.

            But life took a terrible turn!
            One-by-one my loved ones perished—
            First my beloved husband, Elimelech,
            Then both my sons, Mahlon and Chilton.

            Now I am left with only my daughters-in-law,
            Who are not from my land,
                  Eretz Yisrael.

            Hear me, HaShem!
            It is only by your strength that I can go on.
            Only by your grace do I will to see another day.

            Thank you, HaShem!
            Since the famine has ended in Yisrael,
            I will return to the land of my Fathers.

            My daughters, I am returning to my homeland.
            You are still young.
            Go back to your families.
            Find new husbands for yourselves.

Ruth: Naomi tells me to go back
                  to my family in Mo'av,
            But I cannot leave her.

Her God has kept her
Through terrible trials.

Her kindness has comforted me,
    even though I am not
      one of her people.

I will stay with her.
Wherever she goes, I will go.
Her people will be my people.
Her God, Adonai, will be my God.

Ruth, a Gentile,
    took the hem of Naomi's garment
And said to her,
    "I know the Lord is with you."

Faith and a noble character
    shone so brightly in Ruth,
That HaShem noticed.

He honored Ruth
(And Naomi through her)
And placed a king
   in her lineage
    —King David.

But favor did not stop there.
This righteous Gentile's line extended to—
    The King of Kings and Lord of Lords—
      Yeshua Hamashiach!

APPENDIX

RESPONSES TO COMMON JEWISH OBJECTIONS TO NEW COVENANT CLAIMS

Coming from a Jewish background, I have in the past had my own objections to believing in Jesus as the Messiah as well as other claims of the New Covenant.

I would now, not only like to discuss some of those objections, but also point out Old and New Covenant Scripture which can address these issues.

The Trinity

The first objection has to do with the concept of the Trinity.

In Bible times, every nation had its own gods. In Egypt, where the Israelites were slaves for over 400 years, there were many gods. The exodus, subsequent journey through hostile countries, and final settling in the Promised Land, demonstrated that Adonai, the God of Israel was, indeed, Almighty God. Since then, the Jewish people have been known as monotheists--those who believe in one God.

How then can we be reconciled to the concept of an omnipotent, immortal, Triune Godhead? Here are some Scriptures which point to this belief.

In the Shema, the prayer of Moses (Deuteronomy 6:4) it states: "Sh'ma, Yisra'el! ADONAI Eloheinu, ADONAI echad [Hear, Isra'el ADONAI our God, ADONAI is one];" (Complete Jewish Bible). In this verse the word "one" *(echad,* Hebrew) is plural. It actually means "a united entity" such as a bunch of grapes, i.e. several united into one. Similarly, *echad* was used to describe the relationship between a man and his wife when the two become one flesh (Genesis 2:24).

In Genesis 1:1 "In the beginning God created the heavens and the earth" *(NKJV)*, the Hebrew word for "God" is Elohim. Elohim is also plural. The plural connotation of the Godhead is more explicit in Genesis 1:26: "Then God said, let us make man in Our image, according to Our likeness..." *(NKJV)*. Thus, the above verses from the Torah speak of the plural nature of the Godhead.

Now the following Old Covenant Scriptures will testify to the separate identities of the Father, Son and Holy Spirit.

Some verses speak of God's Spirit as a distinct entity. For example, "Then the Lord came down in the cloud, and spoke to him [Moses], and took of the Spirit that was upon him, and placed the same upon the seventy elders; and it happened, when the Spirit rested upon them, that they prophesied, although they never did so again" (Numbers 11:25 NKJV). Later Moses exclaimed, "Oh, that all the Lord's people were prophets and that the Lord would put His Spirit upon them" (Numbers 11:29 NKJV)!

The prophet Isaiah relates that when the Israelites turned from God, "they rebelled and grieved His Holy Spirit" (Isaiah 63:10 *NKJV*). I ask, can one be grieved who does not have a personality?

Old Covenant Scripture about the Son are evident in the following: Proverbs 30:4 says, "Who hath ascended up into heaven and descended? Who hath gathered the wind in His fists? Who hath bound the waters in His garment? Who hath established all the ends of the earth? What is His name, and what is his son's name if thou knowest" (The Masoretic Text)? Then in Psalm 2:7-8 it is prophesied: "I will tell of the decree: The Lord said unto me: 'Thou art My son, This day have I begotten thee. Ask of Me, and I will give the nations for thine inheritance, and the ends of the earth for thy possession'" (The Masoretic Text). Until this proclamation is fulfilled, where is the Son at this time in history? According to David, He is sitting at the right hand of God. Psalm 110:1 says: "The Lord saith unto my lord: 'Sit thou at My right hand, until I make thine enemies thy footstool'" (The Masoretic Text).

In Psalm 16:10 David prophesied that the Son would not be kept in Sheol but would be resurrected: "For Thou wilt not abandon my soul to the nether-world *(Sheol,* Hebrew); Neither wilt Thou suffer thy godly one to see the pit" (The Masoretic Text).

Finally, the following Scriptures speak about God, the Father. Isaiah 63:16 states, "Thou, O Lord, art our Father, Our Redeemer from everlasting is Thy name" (The Masoretic Text). And, "O Lord, Thou are our Father; we are the clay, and Thou our potter" (Isaiah 64:7 The Masoretic Text).

Thus the Father, Son and Holy Spirit *(Ruach Hakodesh,* Hebrew) have been spoken of in the Tanakh (Old Covenant Scriptures). However, it was not until the New Covenant *(B'rit Hadashah,* Hebrew) was established, that Elohim's make-up was more explicitly revealed.

God In The Flesh

Another concept that I, as a Jewess, found difficult to accept is the incarnation of the Son, that is, God appearing in the flesh.

But, according to Scripture, God had appeared several times in human form. Here are two examples. In Genesis 18:1 it says, "ADONAI appeared to Avraham by the oaks of Mamre" (Complete Jewish Bible) and engaged him in conversation. After telling Avraham that he and Sarah will have a child in their old age, "ADONAI said to Avraham, 'Why did Sarah laugh and ask, 'Am I really going to bear a child when I am old?' Is anything too hard for ADONAI'" (Genesis 18:13-14 Complete Jewish Bible)?

Then there is an incredible dialogue, verses 16-32, where ADONAI reasons with Avraham over the fate of Sodom and Gemorrah. No wonder in Isaiah 41:8, ADONAI calls Avraham his "friend"; they had even debated face to face!

An additional example of an incarnation from Genesis occurred when Jacob wrestled with a man the night before he was to be reunited with his brother, Esau (Genesis 32:24-31). Having prevailed in the match, verse 31 says, "Ya'akov called the place P'ni-El [face of God], 'Because I have seen God face to face, yet my life is spared'" (Complete Jewish Bible).

The Suffering Servant

The term Messiah means, Anointed One (Christ, Greek). Why have the Jews been speaking of the Messiah for centuries? It is because prophets, inspired by the Spirit of God, wrote about his coming. They predicted, for example, He would be born in Bethlehem (Micah 5:1); be the seed of Abraham (Genesis 12:3); and be a descendent of David (2 Samuel 7:12-13, Isaiah 11:1-5). In addition, many verses speak of Him as the coming King who will conquer the enemies of Israel, and bring peace on earth. For example, Isaiah 9:6-7 proclaims, "For a child is born to us, a son is given to us; dominion will rest on his shoulders, and he will be given the name Pele-Yo'etz El Gibbor, Avi-' Ad Sar Shalom [Wonder of a Counselor, Mighty God, Father of Eternity, Prince of Peace], in order to extend the dominion and perpetuate the peace of the throne and kingdom of David" (Complete Jewish Bible).

However, Isaiah also speaks of God's servant who will suffer because of the sins of his people.

Isaiah 53:5-6 states, "But he was wounded because of our crimes, crushed because of our sins; the disciplining that makes us whole fell on him, and by his bruises we are healed."

"We all, like sheep, went astray; we turned, each one, to his own way; yet ADONAI laid on him the guilt of all of us" (Complete Jewish Bible).

In verses 11 and 12 of chapter 53, Isaiah concludes, "By His knowing [pain and sacrifice], my righteous servant makes many righteous; it is for their sins that he suffers" (Complete Jewish Bible).

At the time when Yeshua first appeared, the Jewish people were looking for a deliverer to save them from the oppression of the Romans. But, Yeshua's claim, after displaying many miracles, was "My Kingdom is not of this world" (John 18:36 NKJV). His message was one of repentance: to turn the hearts of the Israelite people back to the God of their Fathers. He exhorted, "Turn from your sins to God" (Matthew 4:17 Complete Jewish Bible). However, the people were more interested in the message of the rebel, Barabbas, and chose him to live rather than Yeshua.

Although rejected by his people, nevertheless, Yeshua was willing to be the sacrifice *(kapporah,* Hebrew, "covering") for his people's sin. This fulfilled Isaiah's prophesy, "He is despised and rejected by men" (Isaiah

53:3 NKJV). Isaiah then states, "He was oppressed and He was afflicted, Yet he opened not His mouth; He was led as a lamb to the slaughter... He was taken from prison and from judgment... For he was cut off from the land of the living; For the transgressions of My people He was stricken (Isaiah 53:7-8 *NKJV*). Thus the prophesy concerning the Anointed One's first appearance i.e. to be a sin offering was proclaimed.

This atonement for Israel was accomplished on a hill called Gulgolta, outside Jerusalem, about forty years before the destruction of the temple and the diaspora of the Jewish people. However Yeshua's eternal offering had made it possible for the Jews to have their sins forgiven without the existence of the temple sacrifices.

The New Covenant

Most Jewish people believe there is one covenant established at Mount Sinai between God and the people of Israel. However, the following Scripture recounts something different.

At the Passover *Seder,* the night before Yeshua was hung on the stake, the Scriptures say:

> While they were eating, Yeshua took a piece of *matzah,* made the *b'rakhah,* broke it, gave it to the *talmidim* and said, "Take! Eat! This is my body!" Also he took a cup of wine, made the *b'rakhah,* and gave it to them, saying, "All of you, drink from it! For this is my blood, which ratifies the New Covenant, my blood shed on behalf of many, so that they may have their sins forgiven" (Matthew 26:26-28 Complete Jewish Bible).

Was this concept of a "new" covenant an alien idea to Judaism? The answer is, No. For the prophet Jeremiah, wrote about it in chapter 31, as he declared this future event:

> Behold, the days come, saith the Lord, that I will make a new covenant with the house of Israel, and with the house

of Judah; not according to the covenant that I made with their fathers in the day that I took them by the hand to bring them out of the land of Egypt; forasmuch as they broke My covenant, although I was a lord over them, saith the Lord. But this is the covenant that I will make with the house of Israel after those days, saith the Lord, I will put My law in their inward parts, and in their heart will I write it; and I will be their God, and they shall be My people; and they shall teach no more every man his neighbour, and every man his brother, saying: 'Know the Lord'; for they shall all know Me, from the least of them unto the greatest of them, saith the Lord; for I will forgive their iniquity, and their sin will I remember no more (Jeremiah 31:31-34 The Masoretic Text).

In regard to the covenant established at Mount Sinai, after Moses had read aloud all the laws God had given to the people of Israel and they had agreed to follow them, he took the blood of oxen, the peace offering, and "... sprinkled it on the people and said, 'This is the blood of the covenant which ADONAI has made with you in accordance with all these words'" (Exodus 24:8 Complete Jewish Bible).

However, as Jeremiah says, (see above, Jeremiah 31:31) the Jewish people did not keep the covenant they had made with ADONAI; and a new covenant became necessary which was also instituted with blood. Thus, by the shed blood of Yeshua, the Messiah, for the forgiveness of sins, this new covenant has been ratified and is open to anyone who trusts in Him.

Therefore, just as Moses and Abraham and Jacob had an intimacy with God, once we enter into the New Covenant, we too can know Him in this way as Jeremiah claimed, "For they shall all know Me, from the least of them unto the greatest of them, saith the Lord" (Jeremiah 31:34 The Masoretic Text).

The Resurrection

Another concept difficult to accept is the resurrection of the dead. But the prophets also wrote about this. First, Isaiah in chapter 53:10-12, speaks of the Messiah returning to life to enjoy the reward for going through His agonizing ordeal:

> Yet it pleased the Lord to bruise Him; He has put Him to grief. When You make His soul an offering for sin, He shall see His seed, He shall prolong His days, And the pleasure of the Lord shall prosper in His hand....Therefore I will divide Him a portion with the great, And He shall divide the spoil with the strong, Because He poured out His soul unto death, And He was numbered with the transgressors, And He bore the sin of many, And made intercession for the transgressors (NKJV).

Then in the book of Daniel, chapter 12, it speaks about "the time of the end." An angel is narrating to Daniel the following account: "Many of those sleeping in the dust of the earth will awaken, some to everlasting life and some to everlasting shame and abhorrence" (Daniel 12:2 Complete Jewish Bible). He ends his speech to Daniel with the following encouraging words: "But you, go your way until the end comes. Then you will rest and rise for your reward, at the end of days" (Daniel 12:13 Complete Jewish Bible).

Finally, in Isaiah, chapter 66:23-24, it describes a time when the worshippers of God, and those who have rebelled against Him, will be separated:

> And it shall come to pass, that from one new moon to another, and from one sabbath to another, shall all flesh come to worship before Me, saith the Lord. And they shall go forth, and look upon the carcasses of the men that have rebelled against Me; for their worm shall not die, neither shall their fire be quenched; and they shall be an abhorring unto all flesh (The Masoretic Text).

Types of Messiah

Not only are there hundreds of prophetic Scriptures describing different aspects of the Messiah's life and work to prepare the Jewish people for his coming, God had also pointed to Him through The Writings, the lives of the Patriarchs, and the Passover experience.

The life of Joseph is one example of a type of the Messiah.

Joseph grew up among his brothers. But, after having dreams which pictured him as a ruler over them, they rejected him. In fact, they were so incensed, they decided to kill him. But, his life was spared; and instead, he was sold as a slave.

While a slave in Egypt, he was falsely accused of a crime and put out of sight in jail for years. However, God raised him up, and empowered him supernaturally with the ability to interpret Pharaoh's dreams. Subsequently, he was released from prison and surprisingly, promoted to second in command over all the land of Egypt. Similarly, Yeshua, after being rejected by his people, was abandoned to the grave for three days; but God, raised Him from death and appointed Him to sit at His right hand (Psalm 110:1).

Now, back to Joseph's story. When there was a famine in Canaan, Joseph's brothers came to Egypt for food to keep themselves and their families alive. In Egypt, it was Joseph to whom they had to pay reverence and to whom they went for grain. Did Joseph reject his brothers because of their betrayal years before? No! He forgave and embraced them, and gave them what they needed.

In the same vein, although rejected by many, Yeshua proclaimed, "For the bread of God is He who comes down from heaven and gives life to the world" (John 6:33 *NKJV*). He then continued, "I am the bread of life. He who comes to Me shall never hunger, and he who believes in Me shall never thirst" (John 6:35 NKJV).

Jacob had thought that his son Joseph had been killed as a lad. But, when he realized that Joseph was alive in Egypt, his heart was full. In the same light, one can only imagine the fullness of joy of the Heavenly Father, after the resurrection, and the return of His Son to heaven!

Another type of Messiah is the kind and generous Boaz, in the book of Ruth.

Naomi and her family moved from Israel to Moab during a time of famine. Years later after her husband and sons died, Naomi and her daughter-in-law, Ruth, returned to Bethlehem. Boaz became the kinsman redeemer to Naomi in order to enable her sons' lines of inheritance to continue in Israel. Therefore, he bought their lands and married Mahlon's wife, Ruth "to perpetuate the name of the dead through his inheritance" (Ruth 4:10 NKJV).

Similarly, Yeshua took on flesh, like his kinsmen, so that by the shedding of His blood, He would pay the price set by Elohim for our redemption, guaranteeing our eternal inheritance in the Kingdom of God.

Finally, the Passover lamb is another type of Messiah.

Because Pharaoh refused to let the Israelites leave Egypt to worship God, God struck the country with plagues, as judgment against its various gods. The final plague was the death of the firstborn in every Egyptian household including Pharaoh's, --the firstborn of both children and livestock.

God, however, worked out a plan to spare the Jews. He told them to sacrifice a lamb without blemish, and to spread its blood on the sides and on the top of the door frames of their houses. In this way, when the angel of death came through Egypt, he would pass over the houses with the blood on the doorposts. Thus, the nation of Israel would be spared from the judgment of God (Exodus 12).

In the same manner, those who by faith have the blood of Yeshua spread upon their hearts as a covering for their sins, spiritual death (eternal separation from God) will pass over them. That is why John, the Immerser exclaimed, "Look! God's lamb! The one who is taking away the sin of the world" (John 1:29 Complete Jewish Bible)!

Do we need a sin covering? The Scripture says, "But your iniquities have separated between you and your God" (Isaiah 59:2 The Masoretic Text). And according to Leviticus 17:11, there is only one remedy for sin: "For the life of the flesh is in the blood; and I have given it to you upon the altar to make atonement for your souls" (The Masoretic Text). However without the temple sacrifices, God in His mercy, by His own hand, has dealt a blow to sin and death through the shed blood, and subsequent resurrection of the Messiah. For the Scripture states, "But the fact is that the Messiah has been raised from the dead. The first fruits of those who have died." (I Corinthians 15:20 Complete Jewish Bible). By the resurrection

Isaiah's prophesy, "He will swallow up death forever" (Isaiah 25:8 The Masoretic Text) will be fulfilled.**

Thus, the Passover lamb made it possible for Israel to escape slavery and become a free nation. The Lamb of God, Yeshua, liberates all men from sin and death, and delivers them into the everlasting Kingdom of God.

Messiah as King

There will be a time when the Messiah will rule the earth as King. This was prophesied in Isaiah 9:7, Psalm 2 and Psalm 110.

Since Yeshua fulfilled so many prophesies during His first appearance, there is no doubt that He will come again to fulfill the remaining ones and reign as King over all the earth.

One of the most glorious prophetic words concerning the Kingship of Messiah was given by Daniel in chapter 7:13-14:

> I kept watching the night visions, when I saw, coming with the clouds of heaven, someone like a son of man. He approached the Ancient One and was led into his presence. To him was given rulership, glory and a kingdom, so that all peoples, nations and languages should serve him. His rulership is an eternal rulership that will not pass away; and his kingdom is one that will never be destroyed (Complete Jewish Bible).

At that time, another prophesy will finally be realized: "The stone which the builders rejected is become the chief corner-stone. This is the Lord's doing; It is marvelous in our eyes" (Psalm 118:22-23 The Masoretic Text).

Conclusion

Through Moses, the Prophets, Yeshua and His emissaries, God has been communicating to man about His love, mercy and justice; and it is all

---

** Appendix The Resurrection pages 70-71

recorded in the Bible. And those words can be your joy as it was for Jeremiah when he proclaimed: "Thy words were found, and I did eat them; And Thy words were unto me a joy and the rejoicing of my heart" (Jeremiah 15:16 The Masoretic Text).

The Promised Land

Who was the greatest
      in HaShem's house?
It was Moshe, to whom
      The Law was given.

But alas, it was not
      appointed for him
To bring God's people
      into the Promised Land.

If not the faithful, meek Moshe,
      then who could be found
To courageously lead and to guide
      those twelve chosen clans?

HaShem set apart Joshua, Y'hoshua,
      the son of Nun.
Proclaiming to one and all
      God saves everlastingly.

Joshua led the way—
      by trusting HaShem,
           obeying His word,
                  Jericho's walls couldn't stand!

So too, Yeshua Ha Mashiach,
(God saves through the Anointed One)
      by His obedience,
      brought down the walls—
           the walls of sin and shame—
That we may enter HaShem's presence
      where we,

        by grace,
        can stand!
This is the picture
    HaShem has given:
Following the law will not lead
    to life eternal.

Instead, His hand moving
    through Mashiach Yeshua,
Wrought salvation
    for every woman and man.

Today HaShem is calling:
"Come into the Promised Land.
        enter through the narrow gate
        the rocks now cleared,
        the hills made straight.
Won't you come
    and enter in?"

This is Jerusalem as seen from the Mt. of Olives.
It may be the view Yeshua sees when He returns.

"And His feet shall stand in that day upon the mount of Olives"
(Zechariah 14:4 The Masoretic Text)

All photos were taken either in or just outside of Jerusalem.

The author may be contacted at:
seecooper123@gmail.com

www.ingramcontent.com/pod-product-compliance
Lightning Source LLC
Chambersburg PA
CBHW021450070526
44577CB00002B/344